REGIONAL
WILD AMERICA

UNIQUE ANIMALS OF THE
SOUTHEAST

By Tanya Lee Stone

BLACKBIRCH PRESS
An imprint of Thomson Gale, a part of The Thomson Corporation

THOMSON

GALE

Detroit • New York • San Francisco • San Diego • New Haven, Conn. • Waterville, Maine • London • Munich

For Eileen Cowell, my unique Mom of the Southeast!

Photo Credits: pages 3, 5 (both), 6, 8 Corel; page 7 © Kevin Schafer/CORBIS; page 9 © Lynda Richardson/CORBIS; pages 10, 18, 19 (top) © Joe McDonald/CORBIS; page 11 © W. Perry Conway/CORBIS; page 12 © Joe and Mary McDonald/Visuals Unlimited; page 13 © Lindholm/Visuals Unlimited; pages 14, 22, 23 Photos.com; page 15 Photodisc; page 16 Ralph Lee Hopkins/Lonely Planet Images; page 17 Ray Tipper/Lonely Planet Images; page 19 © Shirley Vanderbilt/Index Stock Imagery; page 20 © Tim Zurowski/CORBIS; page 21 © James Watt/Visuals Unlimited

LIBRARY OF CONGRESS CATALOGING-IN-PUBLICATION DATA

Stone, Tanya Lee.
  Unique animals of the Southeast / by Tanya Lee Stone.
    p. cm. — (Regional wild America)
  Includes bibliographical references and index.
  ISBN 1-56711-969-7 (hard cover : alk. paper)
  1. Animals—Southeastern States—Juvenile literature. I. Title II. Series: Stone, Tanya Lee. Regional wild America.

Printed in the United States of America
10 9 8 7 6 5 4 3 2 1

Contents

The Southeastern United States

NORTH CAROLINA

★ Raleigh

Columbia

★ **SOUTH CAROLINA**

★ Athens

GEORGIA

Atlantic Ocean

★ Tallahassee

Gulf of Mexico

FLORIDA

In the southeastern United States, birds fly, marine life swims, and land animals travel on foot. Many different animals make their homes in the Southeast. When people think of this region, though, they often think of the following animals.

Great blue herons are among the many types of birds that make their home in the wetlands of the southeastern United States.

Radical Reptiles!

The American alligator is the biggest reptile in North America. It is Florida's state reptile and lives in the Southeast. But alligators are also found through Alabama all the way to Texas. In North America, the American crocodile lives only in the Southeast. It lives in swamps and salty bays in southern Florida and the Florida Keys.

Like alligators, crocodiles are very large. They stretch between 7 and 15 feet (2 and 5 m)! They also have powerful jaws and many sharp teeth. One way to tell alligators and crocodiles apart is by the big fourth tooth of each animal. When an alligator's mouth is closed, its large fourth tooth will not show, while a crocodile's will. Another way to tell the difference is that a crocodile has a much narrower snout than an alligator.

Crocodiles are smart animals and excellent hunters. They like to eat fish, turtles, crabs, and some birds. They will also eat almost anything else they can catch and kill! Crocodiles have been known to eat snakes and small mammals.

The American crocodile is endangered, mostly because of loss of habitat. These crocs have also been killed in the past for their skins.

The snout on an American alligator (left) is much wider than a crocodile's (above).

Slinky Skinks

Like crocodiles and alligators, skinks are reptiles. A skink is a kind of lizard. Like other lizards, skinks have claws on the ends of their toes. Skinks have shorter legs than other lizards, and pointier snouts. They also have shiny, overlapping scales. It is clear from its name that the southeastern five-lined skink lives in the Southeast. This medium-sized skink is between 5 and 8 inches long (13 and 20 cm). It mainly eats insects and spiders.

Skinks have shiny, overlapping scales and claws on the ends of their toes.

The bright blue color on the tails of five-lined skinks fades as they get older.

Southeastern five-lined skinks do well in both damp and dry wooded areas. They spend most of their time on the ground, but they are good climbers. Like other skinks, they have a great way of protecting themselves against attackers. If an enemy grabs the skink's tail, its body can break away! The attacker is left holding only the lizard's tail. In time, a new tail grows back.

Young skinks are easily identified by their bright blue tails. As the lizard gets older, the color of its tail fades. The five light-colored stripes down the length of the dark body also fade in males. Males develop a reddish color on their heads during breeding time. Males are slightly larger than females.

Females lay between 4 and 15 eggs in a nest. The group of eggs is called a clutch. Females stay with their eggs until they hatch.

Pocket gophers live in burrows they dig two feet underground.

Pocket Packers

A pocket gopher is a kind of rodent. All rodents have two pairs of incisor teeth. These sharp, chisel-like teeth are used for gnawing and chewing. The teeth grow throughout the animal's life. Rodents have to constantly chew and gnaw things to keep their teeth from getting too big!

Southeastern pocket gophers live in Alabama, Georgia, and Florida. They are between 9 and 12 inches (23 and 31 cm) long. They eat roots, bulbs, and other plant materials. southeastern pocket gophers bother farmers by munching on crop plants such as sweet potatoes, peas, sugarcane, and peanuts.

Like other pocket gophers, these animals dig burrows deep into the ground. The main tunnels are often about 2 feet (0.6 m) under the surface. The tunnels can stretch for 500 feet (153 m)! Deeper pits are also dug that reach 5 feet (1.5 m) underground. These spots are used for nesting, or to store food.

It is easy to spot the burrows by the mounds of dirt the gophers push up to the surface. Large front claws help the pocket gophers dig. They also use their incisors to cut through roots that get in the way.

This young pocket gopher stores flower petals in its cheek pouch until it is ready to eat them later.

Pocket gophers have a unique way of getting food and nesting materials from one place to another. These animals are named for their two cheek pouches, or pockets, on the outside of their body. The fur-lined pockets start at the cheek and go all the way to the shoulder. Pocket gophers pack their pouches full. When they get to wherever they are going, they simply empty their pockets!

Protecting Panthers

Florida's state mammal is the Florida panther. It is a kind of cougar. This sleek cat is endangered. This means it is in danger of becoming extinct and is protected by law. These cats were once found from Texas all the way east to South Carolina. Now they are only found in small areas of Florida. Before 1900, many of them were killed by hunters. Since then, loss of habitat has been their main problem.

Florida panthers live in swampy forests and woodlands. They are good swimmers and can easily cross canals and marshes. They average 6 to 7 feet (1.8 to 2 m) in length. They weigh between 66 and 145 pounds (30 and 65 kg). There are two things that make the Florida panther different from all other cougars. Midway down its back, the Florida panther has a twirl of hair that stands out from the rest of its fur pattern. And the end of its long tail has a bend, or turn, in it.

These large cats are carnivores. This means they are meat eaters. Their favorite food is the white-tailed deer. They also hunt wild hogs, rabbits, raccoons, and birds. Like other large cats, the Florida panther is an excellent hunter. It quietly and slowly stalks its prey. When it is in striking distance, it quickly pounces!

Today, there are only between eighty and one hundred of these animals in the wild. There are several efforts to help them. Preserving their habitat and teaching people about the importance of protecting these cats are great ways to help. There is hope that in time, the panther population in Florida will grow again.

Florida panthers are excellent hunters and stalk their prey through the swampy forests and woodlands where they live.

Bottlenose dolphins are very social marine mammals and communicate with each other using a complex system of whistles.

Dazzling Dolphins!

The bottlenosed dolphin swims in warm waters throughout the world. It can be seen off the coast of Florida year-round. It also travels as far north as North Carolina in the summertime. These marine mammals are very social and intelligent. They live in groups and seem to have a complex system of communicating with each other. Scientists believe that each dolphin has its own unique whistle, much like every human has a unique voice.

Bottlenosed dolphins are meat eaters that feed on fish, shrimp, squid, and eels. Like bats, they use echolocation to find food. They send out sounds that hit objects and then bounce back to their ears—like an echo. The echoes tell the dolphin where an object is. They also tell the dolphin how big something is and how fast it is traveling. This amazing talent is called echolocation.

These animals weigh about 350 to 600 pounds (159 to 272 kg). They can even weigh up to 1,400 pounds (635 kg)! Their bodies stretch from 7 to 12 feet (2 to 4 m) long. They are graceful swimmers. A bottlenosed dolphin often swims between 7 and 10 miles (11 and 16 km) per hour.

Dolphins find food under water by using echolocation.

Big-Billed Birds

Because they fly, birds often have a wider range of territory than other animals. But within the United States, the wood stork breeds only in parts of the Southeast. There are nest sites in Florida, Georgia, and South Carolina. Wood storks build big nests in trees found in swampy areas or on islands. They are large wading birds with long legs. Wood storks stand between 40 and 44 inches (102 and 112 cm) tall. Their wings stretch 60 to 65 inches (152 to 165 cm). A wood stork's head is black, while most of its body is white.

This bird has a large and heavy bill that makes it easy to identify. A wood stork looks for food by poking its bill in the water until it finds a fish. Then it snatches up its meal in a flash! The wood stork is endangered. This is mostly due to loss of habitat.

Wood storks are endangered because humans have destroyed many of the wetlands where they feed and breed.

The glossy ibis is another bird that tends to stick to the Southeast—at least in the winter months. In the summer, it is also found along the East Coast. The glossy ibis is smaller than the wood stork. It stands about 23 inches (58 cm) tall. Like the wood stork, this wading bird has a large, long beak. And it uses it to feed in a similar way. But its food choices are different. The glossy ibis pokes its bill into shallow waters to find crabs, crayfish, insects, and snakes! This bird is well named for its glossy green wings. Its body feathers are a reddish brown.

The glossy ibis likes to eat crabs, crayfish, and snakes and uses its curved bill to pull them out of shallow water.

Pretending to Be Poisonous!

Several kinds of snakes live in the Southeast. Three of the snakes in this region are related in an interesting way. One of them is poisonous. But the other two only look as if they are! That is because the scarlet snake and the scarlet kingsnake have markings to look like the poisonous eastern coral snake. This is called mimicry. It is one way animals have of protecting themselves. Even though scarlet snakes are not poisonous, their markings signal enemies to stay away.

The markings on a scarlet snake protect it by making it look like a poisonous eastern coral snake.

All three of these reptiles have bandlike markings. The scarlet and scarlet kingsnake have red and yellow markings separated by black. The eastern coral has the same colors, but its red and yellow rings are next to each other. This is important to remember because the eastern coral is very dangerous and should never be touched. There is even a saying to remind people which snake to avoid. It is, "Red touch yellow, kill a fellow. Red and black, friend of Jack."

The scarlet snakes are close in size. Scarlet kingsnakes are between 14 and 27 inches (36 and 69 cm) long. The scarlet snake stretches between 14 and 32 inches (36 and 81 cm) in length. The eastern coral is a bit bigger at 20 to 47 inches (51 to 119 cm). It attacks and eats snakes and lizards. Scarlet snakes eat other snakes, too. They also eat small lizards and rodents. All three snakes spend much of their time hiding under logs or in leaves.

The harmless scarlet kingsnake (top) looks similar to the poisonous and very dangerous eastern coral snake (below).

Softshells and Sea Shells

A turtle is another type of reptile. Two kinds of turtles are well known in the Southeast. They are the Florida softshell turtle and the loggerhead turtle.

Most turtles have top shells that are hard. Softshell turtles get their name from the soft, leathery skin that covers their top shells. There are only three kinds of softshell turtles that live in North America. One of them is the Florida softshell. It lives in ponds, rivers, and lakes. Its webbed feet make it a good swimmer. These freshwater turtles also have pointy noses for poking into cracks and crevices while looking for food. They like to eat fish, frogs, crayfish, and snails. Florida softshell turtles can get around on land just as well as in the water. Females are usually bigger than males. A female can be up to 20 inches (51 cm) long. Males are often about 13 inches (33 cm) long.

The Florida softshell turtle is a good swimmer and lives in the water, but it can also get around well on land.

The loggerhead sea turtle is South Carolina's state reptile. The loggerhead is a threatened animal. There are not as many of them as there used to be. Loggerhead turtles are found in warm waters throughout many parts of the world. The Southeast is home to several nesting sites for these animals. Loggerheads only nest every two to three years, so it is important to protect these sites.

Loggerheads can weigh up to 350 pounds (159 kg) and be 40 inches (102 cm) long. They have strong jaws. This helps them eat shelled animals such as clams, mussels, and horseshoe crabs. Like other sea turtles, loggerheads have flippers instead of legs. They are excellent swimmers and move easily through the water. When females come ashore to nest, though, they have to drag their heavy bodies slowly across the sand.

A loggerhead turtle's flippers help it move easily through the water.

Mild-Mannered Manatees

Like the dolphin, the Florida manatee is a marine mammal. But it rarely goes into deep ocean waters. This animal swims off the coast of Florida. Although it may travel as far north as Virginia, it usually stays in the south where waters are warmest. The Florida manatee is endangered.

Manatees are large animals. They are about 10 feet (3 m) long. They often weigh between 800 and 1,100 pounds (363 and 499 kg). Some can even weigh up to 3,500 pounds (1,589 kg). Females are usually bigger than males.

Manatees are herbivores. This means that they are plant eaters. They eat many kinds of water plants, such as grasses, mangrove leaves, and algae. These gentle animals spend their days mainly resting and feeding. They also spend some time with other manatees. Manatees can sometimes be seen diving together or playing what looks like a follow-the-leader kind of game.

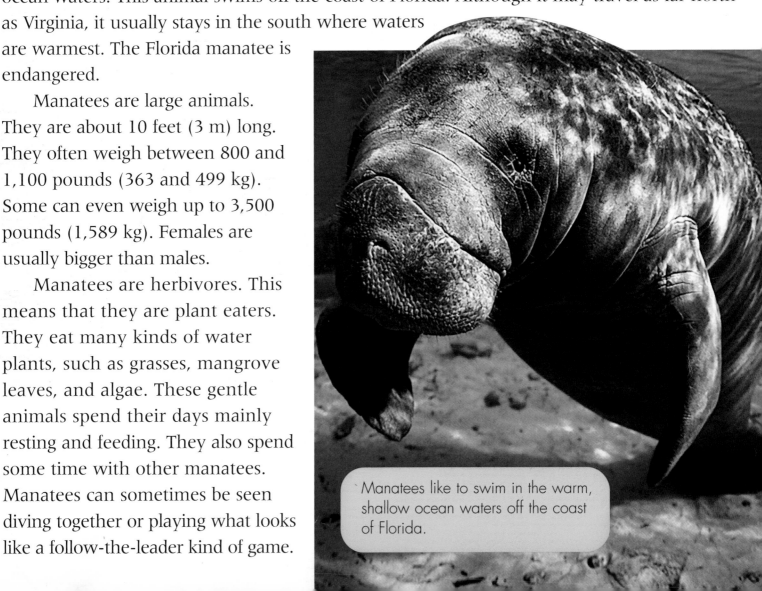

Manatees like to swim in the warm, shallow ocean waters off the coast of Florida.

Like other marine animals, a manatee's body is well shaped for swimming. Its wide tail looks like a paddle. The tail moves up and down, sending the animal through the water. Its front flippers help a manatee steer. It does not have back flippers. Manatees often cruise through the water at a calm 2 to 5 miles (3 to 8 km) per hour. They can speed up to 15 miles (24 km) per hour.

Manatees have small eyes and can see very well underwater. When they need to breathe, they poke their nostrils above the surface. A manatee usually surfaces for air every 2 to 3 minutes. They can stay underwater up to 20 minutes

Manatees feed on grasses, leaves, water plants, and algae.

There are many unique and wonderful animals that live in the Southeast. All of them add to the richness and beauty of this region.

Glossary

Carnivore An animal that mainly eats meat.
Clutch Group of eggs.

Echolocation Locating objects using echoes.
Herbivore An animal that mainly eats plants.

For More Information

Eckart, Edana. *Bottlenose Dolphin.* Danbury, CT: Children's Press, 2003.

Ricciuti, Edward. *What on Earth is a Skink?* San Diego, CA: Blackbirch Press, 1994.

Staub, Frank. *Manatees.* Minneapolis, MN: Lerner, 1998.

Stone, Tanya Lee. *Crocodilians.* San Diego, CA: Blackbirch Press, 2003.

Index